Cambridge English Readers

Level 2

Series editor: Philip Prowse

Different Worlds

Margaret Johnson

T0094898

CAMBRIDGE
UNIVERSITY PRESS

CAMBRIDGE
UNIVERSITY PRESS

University Printing House, Cambridge CB2 8BS, United Kingdom

One Liberty Plaza, 20th Floor, New York, NY 10006, USA

477 Williamstown Road, Port Melbourne, VIC 3207, Australia

314–321, 3rd Floor, Plot 3, Splendor Forum, Jasola District Centre, New Delhi – 110025, India

79 Anson Road, #06–04/06, Singapore 079906

Cambridge University Press is part of the University of Cambridge.

It furthers the University's mission by disseminating knowledge in the pursuit of education, learning and research at the highest international levels of excellence.

www.cambridge.org
Information on this title: www.cambridge.org/9780521536554

© Cambridge University Press 2003

First published 2003
Reprinted 2019

Printed in the United Kingdom by Hobbs the Printers Ltd.

A catalogue record for this publication is available from the British Library

ISBN 978-0-521-53655-4 Paperback

Illustrations by Kathryn Baker

Contents

People in the story

Sam: a young deaf girl
Sam's mum
Ron: Sam's best friend
Jim
Lauren: Jim's ex-girlfriend

Chapter 1 *A hand on a guitar*

Before I was born, my mum played music with four friends. There's a photograph of them in our living room. Evie, Grace, Angela, Kate and my mum. They were the Sweet Pepper Band, and they played South American music. Mum played guitar.

Mum had long dark hair. In the photograph she's wearing a big hat, a red shirt and yellow trousers. She looks South American, but she's not, she's English. She's smiling in the photograph. She looks beautiful.

She's beautiful now too. But these days her hair is short and the dark brown colour comes from a bottle. Mum doesn't play her guitar very often any more. It sits in the corner of the living room waiting for Evie, Grace, Angela or Kate to visit.

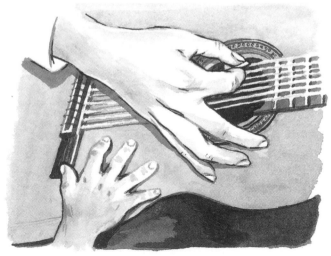

When I was a little girl, I liked to put my small hand on the front of Mum's guitar while she played it. My hand moved a little because of the music. Mum said that was called vibration. She was happy that I could feel the vibration of her music when I put my hand on her guitar. And she wasn't angry when one day I had blue paint on my hand and I put it on the guitar.

Mum liked me to feel the vibration of her music, you see. That's because I can't hear her music. My ears don't work. I'm deaf. I was born like that. Sometimes I think that's why Mum doesn't play music very often, because she knows I can't hear it. And now that I'm eighteen years old, my hands are too big to put them on the front of the guitar.

I don't know if Mum was sad to have a deaf baby. She tells me I was beautiful when I was born. I had lots of blonde hair and blue eyes that went brown like hers after a few months. But I don't think Mum's sad because she smiles all the time.

Mum smiles more than anyone I know. She's always happy, that's one of the things everyone loves about her. The children at Busy Kids Day Nursery, where we both work, all love Mum. Busy Kids is Mum's business. She started it five years ago.

Mum's really good with children. I remember when I was quite young – five or six years old – I was sad about something. I don't remember what I was sad about, but I do remember what Mum said. We sat in a chair together with her face close to mine and she put her arms around me. We stayed like that for a while, and then she sat back so she could talk to me. Mum and I use our hands and fingers to talk to each other. It's called signing.

Anyway, Mum said that we can choose how to be in life
– happy or sad. She said, 'Life's short, so choose to be
happy.' I try never to forget those words.

I try to be like my mum because I think she's a
wonderful person. I don't know much about my father
because he left after I was born. All I know is that he played
music too, and that he's French. He lives in Paris now.

Mum and my father met when he was working in
Norwich for a year. They fell in love and soon got married.
Dad moved into the house where Mum and I live now.
Norwich is a beautiful place, but it isn't as big and exciting
as Paris. I think my father got bored. Or perhaps he was
sad when I was born deaf. Because that's when he went
away to live with his family in Paris. He never came back.

Some of my friends don't talk to their parents very
much. My friend Suzanne sometimes tells her mother she's

with me when she's really with her boyfriend. She does this because her mum worries about her all the time. She worries about where she is and who she's with. But Mum and I are very close, and I couldn't tell her something that wasn't true. Anyway, she doesn't worry the way Suzanne's mum does, so I usually tell her everything.

But I didn't tell her when I fell in love for the first time.

I don't know why. Perhaps it was because it felt so strange; because *I* felt so strange. It was almost like being on a boat on an angry sea. Sometimes I was afraid of how I felt.

And there was another problem. I didn't know the name of the man I was in love with.

Chapter 2 *Shopping*

Just for a moment, try to think what it's like to live in my world. Stop what you're doing and put your hands over your ears. Are there no sounds at all? Or are the noises of the street just quieter than usual?

I know Mum loves listening to the sounds of birds singing in the countryside when we go walking. In my world there are no birds singing. There are no noisy men working on the roads. No people leaving bars late at night shouting at each other. No babies crying.

But the man I love doesn't live in my world. He lives in the hearing world.

The first time I saw him, he was standing in front of the shop across the road from our house. He was putting apples and oranges onto the table outside the shop and his black hair had blue lights in it from the sun.

I watched him from my bedroom window, and I smiled at how carefully he was putting the fruit onto the table. He was like an artist, not a shop assistant. Then, as I watched, a big motorbike went up the street. The young man looked up and smiled as he watched it go past. I *saw* the motorbike go past, but he heard it first, *then* saw it.

After the motorbike was gone, he went back to his fruit. But then a small girl fell off her bicycle close to the shop and he ran to help her. He knew she wanted help because he heard her.

In only one minute, I already knew four things about him.

He had beautiful black hair.

He liked motorbikes.

He was kind to apples, oranges and little girls.

And, of course, he could hear.

Until I first saw him, I didn't think very often about being deaf. It's all I've ever known, and I can't do anything to change it. And all my boyfriends have been deaf. But after I saw the young man, I wanted to be like most other people. I didn't want to be different.

I soon found out that he only worked at the shop on Saturdays. After that I went in there to buy something each Saturday. Every week I wanted to talk to him, but every week I just smiled and paid for my things. Things that I didn't really want.

Mum often looked at me strangely when I came back from the shop. 'We didn't need any apples, Samantha,' she said once. 'I bought some yesterday.' And another time, 'We've already got biscuits in the cupboard.'

On Saturdays I always wanted to go to the shop, but I

always felt afraid too. I never felt very comfortable as I walked across the road. I played with the money in my pocket like a child going to buy sweets. And then sometimes when I got to the shop I waited for a moment outside, reading the postcards in the window. People who want to sell things write about them on a postcard and the young man puts them in the window: 'Car, five years old', 'Cat needs good home', 'Large fridge, nearly new'.

One Saturday I read all of the postcards twice before I went into the shop. Then, when I was inside, I didn't know what to buy. Mum and I always go to the supermarket on Fridays and I really didn't want anything. The young man was busy selling bread and cakes to a woman with two children. This gave me time to think, and in the end I decided to buy a newspaper.

The shop was often very busy on Saturdays. Usually the young man just had time to smile at me and take my money. But that morning it was different. After the woman and her children left, the shop was empty. There was only me and the young man.

When I took my newspaper to him to pay for it, he smiled. But when I tried to smile back at him, my mouth felt like wood. Then he said something to me. I watched his mouth closely. We had lessons at school to help us lip-read – to watch people's mouths to read their words when they talk. I can lip-read quite well. So I watched the young man's mouth and I thought he was talking about a fire. A big fire. Then I looked down at my newspaper and saw a picture of a house on fire.

It was a colour picture, and the fire was very big and red. I hoped nobody was in the house.

That's what I wanted to say to the young man: 'How terrible! I hope nobody was in the house.' But I didn't say it. I didn't say anything. I don't like speaking, you see. I don't like actually using my voice. When I was a child I often tried to talk and other children didn't understand me. Sometimes they laughed. That's why I think my voice sounds strange. And I didn't want the young man to think I was strange.

When I looked up, the young man was speaking again. Then he waited for me to answer him. But I didn't hear him, so I couldn't. So I just smiled and took my newspaper and left the shop.

But as I walked across the road to my house, I felt sad because I was sure he probably *did* think I was strange now.

Chapter 3   *My best friend*

Mum looked at me when I went into the house with the newspaper. We signed to each other.

'Are you OK?' she asked, and I did my best to smile.

'Yes, I'm OK,' I said.

She looked at me for a moment as if she didn't quite believe me, and then she said, 'Ron's here. He's in the living room.'

That made me happy again. Ron is my very best friend. We lived next door to each other when we were children. Now he's a student in London, and I don't get to see him very often. He's studying to be a teacher of deaf children. He wanted to become one because of me. Ron learnt to speak to me by signing when he was very young.

I went quickly into the living room. Ron was sitting on the sofa reading a magazine. When he saw me he put the magazine down. 'Hi, Sam!' he signed to me and smiled.

'Hi, Ron.' I smiled back and kissed him. 'How are you?' I was really happy to see him. I knew I could tell him about my problem with the man from the shop. Ron understood these things. I remember the first time he fell in love. It was with my friend Suzanne, actually.

Mum put her head round the door. I watched her mouth move as she asked Ron if he wanted a cup of tea. She likes Ron as much as I do. When we were children, she often took both of us to the sea for the day.

Once I asked Ron what the sound of the sea was like. He

said, 'The sea's loud when it gets to the beach. But it can be soft and quiet too.'

Usually I don't feel sad about being deaf, but I love the sea, and I would like to hear what it sounds like very much.

I quickly told Ron about the man from the shop before Mum came back with the tea.

'Actually, I think I know him,' Ron said after a few moments. 'My brother's friend has a Saturday job at that shop. He's a student at the university. He lives in Pete's house.'

Pete is Ron's brother. I couldn't believe it! my man lived in Pete's house! 'What's his name?' I asked.

'Jim,' Ron told me. 'Actually, Pete's having a party at his house tonight. Come with me. Jim will probably be there.'

Parties are difficult for me because I can't talk to people. It's different when I'm with my other deaf friends because we sign to each other and we laugh a lot. Going to a party with them is different to going to any other sort of party. We all speak the same language. When I'm at a party with them, I'm in the centre of things. At parties with hearing people, I'm on the outside. Or I *feel* as if I am.

Ron knew what I was thinking. 'Come to the party,' he signed. 'Please. I'd like you to come.'

'OK,' I said at last, just as Mum came in with the tea.

Chapter 4   *The party*

Later I was looking at all my clothes when Mum came into my bedroom. I had a green dress in one hand and a short black skirt in the other hand. I wasn't happy with the dress or the skirt.

Mum took a blue jumper from the bed and gave it to me. 'The weather man on the television says that it will snow,' she said. Then she smiled and kissed me, and I felt bad that she didn't know about Jim. I decided to tell her as soon as there was anything to tell. *If* there was anything to tell.

It was almost spring, but it was still very cold. Ron and I stopped to buy some drinks on the way to the party and by the time we got to Pete's house it was beginning to snow.

Ron looked at me as we waited at the door. 'OK?' he asked.

I smiled at him. 'Yes,' I said, 'I'm OK.'

A girl opened the door and said hello to Ron. I didn't know her. She was very pretty and she was wearing a nice red dress. I smiled at her and followed Ron into the house.

Inside, we went into the kitchen. It was full of people. All the girls were wearing short dresses or skirts. I was the only one wearing a jumper and jeans.

Ron and I took our drinks into the living room. This room was full of people too. And it was hot – very hot – but I couldn't take my jumper off because I wasn't wearing a T-shirt under it. The jumper was a mistake, but I tried to forget about it.

'The music's very loud,' I said to Ron.

'How do you know that?' he asked and smiled.

'Because I can feel it in my legs,' I told him, and it was true. It was like my hand on Mum's guitar. The vibration of the music was travelling from the floor into my feet. Then it was going right up my legs and into my body.

A man came up to us. It was Pete. He said something to Ron, then looked right at me. Pete knows I'm deaf of course. 'Hello, Sam,' I saw his mouth saying.

'Where's Jim?' I wanted to ask, but I didn't. I just said hello and smiled. Pete talked to us for a while, then he went to change the music. Ron talked to me. People in the room watched us talking with our hands. People often watch when I use sign language. It's interesting for them, I think.

Ron told me about the fun he was having with his new friends in London. He talked a lot about a girl called Mary.

'Is Mary your girlfriend?' I asked him, and his face went a bit red.

'At the moment she's just a friend,' he said. 'But I want her to be my girlfriend.'

I thought about Jim. Where was he? Why wasn't he here? The party was in his house!

Ron often knows what I'm thinking. 'He'll come soon,' he told me.

Around ten o'clock, Ron was talking to some other friends across the room. I felt very hot in my jumper, so I decided to go into the garden for a short time.

Outside, everything was white. There was snow everywhere, and it was beautiful. The garden looked like a big white cake, and I was the first person to walk on it.

Or, I thought I was the first person to walk on it. But after a few moments I saw that I wasn't. I could see empty places in the snow made by shoes – footprints. But I couldn't see anyone.

But I knew someone was there because just then something very cold hit the side of my face. Snow!

Chapter 5 *Snow fun*

More snowballs flew past my face. Then I saw someone come out from behind a white tree. It was the man from the shop! It was Jim!

I laughed and quickly made a snowball. Then I sent it through the air.

But Jim moved so quickly to one side the snowball hit a tree behind him. So I started to make another snowball, but before it was ready, Jim threw a new one at me.

I laughed again. Then I ran behind a wall and made lots of snowballs. When they were ready, I came out from behind the wall. But Jim had made lots of snowballs too, and soon I was very wet.

After a few minutes I was laughing so much my stomach hurt, just the way it does when I'm laughing at parties with my deaf friends.

When I looked up at last, I saw that Jim was standing quite close to me. I also saw that something was wrong. He wasn't smiling now. He was looking at me. I remembered how he looked at me in the shop and I knew it was the same now. He was waiting for me to answer him. But I couldn't.

I looked into his face, waiting for him to speak again. After a while, he did, and this time I watched his mouth very carefully. There was an outside light on the side of the house. Anyway, the snow all around us made it almost as light as day.

'What's your name?' he asked. This time I knew it was very important for me say something.

'Sam,' I said carefully. 'My name's Sam. Samantha.' Then I told him: 'I can't hear what you say. I'm deaf.'

He looked at me for a very long time, and I wasn't sure if he understood. Then he smiled. 'Can you lip-read, Sam?' he asked.

I nodded. 'Yes,' I said. 'Usually.'

'Then lip-read this,' he said, moving his mouth carefully. 'The time for talking has finished. Get your snowballs ready!' Then he ran away and went back behind his tree. Before I could move, snowballs were coming through the air again.

I ran back behind my wall, laughing. My first snowball hit him in the face. But he sent one back which got me on my face. The snow was cold and wet in my eyes, but I didn't mind. I was happy. I knew Jim was throwing snowballs at me because he liked me.

Sometimes when people learn about me being deaf they're very careful with me. I feel like I'm a piece of expensive glass. It's difficult to be friends with a piece of expensive glass. But Jim wasn't careful with me, and I liked that.

Soon I was very hot. But I didn't want to stop. I wanted to throw snowballs at Jim all night. But after about five minutes, Jim stopped. When I looked over to see why, I saw his mouth was moving. But he wasn't looking at me, he was looking at someone behind me. I turned and saw a girl standing near the house. It was the girl in the red dress. The same girl who opened the door when Ron and I arrived at the party. She was saying something to Jim and she didn't look happy. She wasn't smiling and her eyes were cold. As cold as her legs in the short red dress.

Jim started to walk across the snowy grass. When he got near to me, he smiled and looked into my face. 'I'll win next time,' he said, then he went inside with the girl.

I stayed on in the garden for a few minutes more, but it wasn't much fun now. You can't really throw snowballs at yourself.

When I went back in the house I found Ron in the kitchen.

'Sam! You're still here,' he signed. 'I was looking for you.' He looked at my wet clothes. 'What happened to your jumper?'

Before I could answer I saw Jim on the other side of the kitchen. The girl in the red dress was talking to him, but he wasn't listening. He was watching me and Ron speaking with our hands.

Ron saw who I was looking at. 'Have you been outside with Jim?' he asked, and he smiled when my red face gave him my answer.

'I've been with Jim and about a hundred snowballs.' I smiled as I signed the words.

Ron laughed. More people came into the kitchen and he moved closer to me. There wasn't enough room for him to sign now, so he spoke carefully. 'It's very good to see you, Sam,' he said. 'I like London, but it's not so much fun without you there.'

Ron is like my brother. So when he kissed my face, I knew it was the kiss of a brother to his sister.

But I didn't know if Jim knew that.

Chapter 6 *Spring cleaning*

The next Saturday was the first Saturday in March. Mum always likes us to clean the house on the first Saturday in March. She calls it spring cleaning. She was cleaning downstairs, and I was cleaning upstairs. I wanted to be upstairs because I could see the shop from my bedroom window. Downstairs there are always cars in the street outside and you can't see out very well.

I really wanted to see Jim again, and I looked out of the window often while I was cleaning. Once he came outside

to put some fruit and flowers onto the table, but he didn't look across the road.

The snowball fight was a week ago now. A week is a long time if you're in love. It was sunny and the snow was gone now. I was sorry about that.

'Haven't you finished this room, Sam?' Mum stood in front of me, signing. She couldn't understand why I was still cleaning my room. I'm usually quite quick at cleaning. When I'm not looking out of windows and remembering snowballs.

'Sorry,' I answered, and she smiled.

'That's OK. Actually, can you go to the shop to get a bottle of window cleaner for me? I forgot to buy some.'

I couldn't believe it! She was sending me to the shop! 'Do you feel OK, Sam?' Mum asked me. 'You look hot.'

'Yes,' I answered. 'I feel fine.' But I knew my face was red.

'Are you sure?' she said. 'I'll go to the shop if you want.'

'No!' I signed. 'I'll go.' And I quickly went downstairs and left the house.

Jim was busy when I went into the shop. He was standing near the bottles of wine with a man. He was helping the man to decide which wine to buy. The man was quite short. Jim smiled at me over his head.

I smiled at him, and then I went over to the bottles of cleaner. Mum always buys the same window cleaner, but I stood in front of the different bottles as if I didn't know which one was best. I wanted the short man to choose his wine quickly and leave. I wanted Jim to myself.

At last the man left, carrying two bottles of wine, one red, one white. I took my window cleaner over to Jim to pay for it. When I got there he was writing something on a piece of paper. Then he gave it to me. The writing was large and black. It was like an artist's writing. I read the words: 'I know more about snowballs than wine.'

I laughed.

'Did you enjoy our snowball fight?' he wrote next.

I took the pen from him. 'Yes,' I wrote, 'I did. Very much.' After he'd read my words, he looked at me. Then he started writing again.

'Is Ron your boyfriend?' I read.

This time I didn't write, I spoke. 'No,' I said. 'He's my best friend. I haven't got a boyfriend.'

Jim understood me without any problem. Or I think he did, because he smiled. 'Do you want to meet me tomorrow night?' he said, and he moved his mouth carefully so I could lip-read his words.

'Yes,' I said. 'I'd like that.'

'How long does it take to buy window cleaner, Sam?' Mum asked me when I got back to the house, but I only smiled.

'Sorry, Mum,' I signed and hurried quickly upstairs.

It wasn't until I started cleaning Mum's bedroom that I thought about the girl in the red dress again. Who was she? But I was afraid of the answer. I liked Jim too much and I didn't want to think about the girl in the red dress.

Chapter 7   *A new boyfriend*

Next day, Mum and I went to Winterton for a walk. Winterton is one of my favourite places. It's east of Norwich, by the sea. Winterton is where Mum took me and Ron when we were children. It takes about forty-five minutes to drive there. We put on our coats and made some coffee and some sandwiches to take with us.

On the beach it was cold but sunny. Some children were running by the sea with their dog. As we walked along, I told Mum about Jim.

When I was finished, my face was a bit red. 'You really like him, don't you?' she said, looking at me.

It was windy by the sea. Mum's hair was all over her face, but I could see her smile through it.

'Yes,' I said, 'I do.'

Just for a moment, she looked a little sad. She walked ahead a short way, then she looked back at me. 'Love is wonderful,' she said, smiling again. 'Enjoy it while you can, Sam. Enjoy it while you can.'

I did enjoy myself that evening. Very much.

Jim and I went to a bar in the centre of Norwich. It was in the old area of town, close to the river. There was a pool table in the bar. I like playing pool. Ron taught me how to play, years ago. Now I'm better than him.

Jim saw me looking at the pool table and the next moment he was putting some money into the side of it. We played and I won easily. It only took five minutes.

My last boyfriend got angry when he lost. But when I looked at Jim I saw that he was laughing. I liked that.

'Very good!' he said. 'But my snowballs are better than yours!' Then he looked at me. 'Can you understand me?'

I smiled. 'Yes,' I said. 'I can understand if you speak slowly. Can you understand me?'

Jim smiled too. 'Yes,' he said, 'I can understand you very well.'

We sat down together at a table and for the next two hours we talked. Most of the time we spoke to each other, and sometimes we wrote things down. I didn't think about

27

how we were talking. I was too interested in what we were saying.

This was what I found out about Jim. He was twenty-one years old and he was studying English at university in Norwich. This was his last year as a student. His family lived in Derbyshire, in the middle of England. He had a brother of twenty-five, a sister of seventeen and a dog called Sky. He liked walking in the hills near his family home. He told me that in winter the hills were often white with snow. Winter was his favourite time. Then he told me the only two things he didn't like about Norfolk: there weren't many hills and it didn't snow very often!

Mum has told me that people who live in different places in England sound different when they speak. People from Derbyshire sound different to people from London, and people from London sound different to people from Norwich. They have different accents. So I knew that Jim probably had a different accent to the other people around us in the bar.

Then Jim wanted to know about me, so I told him about my job at Busy Kids. I said that I spent a lot of my time playing, and that the children don't mind about me being deaf. 'I won't always work at Busy Kids,' I finished. 'I like working there but I also like writing stories. One day I want to write a book.'

'I'm sure you will,' Jim said. 'You'll write a book and you'll be famous.'

'I just want to be happy,' I wrote on his piece of paper. But I was already happy. Happy being with Jim.

'What's it like to be deaf?' Jim asked then, and I thought for a moment.

'You don't mind me asking you that, do you?' Jim asked.

'No,' I wrote. 'I want to tell you. But it's difficult.'

'I think it must be very peaceful,' Jim said. 'I like noise, but sometimes I need to be quiet. That's when I go to the countryside for a walk.' He laughed. 'But actually the countryside can be a very noisy place! There are cars and animals and birds singing . . .'

'Mum likes listening to the birds sing,' I told him.

'Yes, I do too.' he said. 'And the sound of the wind in the trees . . .'

'Sometimes my world is too quiet,' I said, and Jim touched my hand.

'Don't be sad,' he said, and I smiled.

'I'm not sad,' I said, and it was true. I was very happy, being with Jim. 'I think being deaf is a bit like swimming underwater,' I told him. 'You know, when you're swimming and you look up through the water. Everything looks different. The water changes everything.'

Jim moved his chair near to mine and took my hand in his. 'Fish always live in the water,' he said. 'It's all they know.'

'Yes,' I said, and I knew he understood what I was trying to tell him. 'Fish don't know that the water makes things look different.'

When the bar closed, Jim walked home with me. He had his bicycle with him. It was dark, so I couldn't read his lips, but I didn't mind. It was nice just to be with him. We lived in different worlds because I was deaf, and he wasn't. But it wasn't important.

Outside my house, we stopped under a street light. Jim

looked into my eyes. 'What's your mobile phone number? So I can text you.'

I told him my mobile phone number. Then I showed him how to say goodbye in sign language. He tried it a few times. Then, he showed me another way to say goodbye. With a kiss.

I liked that way best.

Chapter 8 *The girl in the red dress*

That evening was the beginning of something wonderful, because Jim and I met often after that. Sometimes he went out with his friends or stayed at home to study. But we saw each other as often as we could.

We met in cafés or in bars, or we just went for walks. Sometimes we used pen and paper to talk, but usually I read his lips. I showed him some more sign language too. But often we didn't have to talk at all. We just liked being together. When we weren't together we sent each other text messages and emails. In this way we spoke to each other every day. Sometimes I felt I was living a dream, a very good dream. I was in love and I was very happy.

Until the day I met the girl in the red dress again. The girl from the party.

It was a Monday morning and I was on my way to work. Mum had left early to meet a new parent, so I was walking. It was a sunny day, and I was feeling good. I went to the shops to buy food for the children's lunches and then I walked through the park. I was probably thinking about Jim, because I was always thinking about Jim.

I didn't see the girl with the red dress until she stood in front of me. She wasn't wearing a red dress that day, of course, but I knew who she was.

'Hello,' I said, but she didn't say anything. She just stood there and looked at me. Then, when she started speaking, she talked really quickly. Too quickly.

'Please,' I said. 'Can you speak more slowly? I can't understand you.'

She looked cross. 'What?' I saw her say. 'I can't understand you!'

My face went red, but I tried again, speaking carefully. 'Please speak more slowly so I can read your lips. I'm deaf.'

When she spoke again, she spoke very slowly. Too slowly. I could understand every word. 'Jim was *my* boyfriend before he met you,' she said. '*My* boyfriend. We were very happy together. Very happy. I'm good for him in a way you can never be good for him. How can you be good for him? You can't hear his music!'

'His music?' I didn't understand what she meant.

She looked at me. 'Don't you know about his music?' she said. 'Jim plays in a band! I can't believe you don't know that! The band means everything to him. *Everything.* And he needs to be with someone who can hear his music. Jim writes songs. Didn't you know that? You really don't know Jim very well, do you? He writes songs and he plays them to me before he tries them with the band. He could never do that with you, could he? So stay away from him, understand? You'll never make him happy the way I do.'

She waited for a moment to see if I would say anything, but I was too hurt inside to speak. Hurt and afraid. So she said it one more time: 'Stay away from Jim.' Then she left.

There was a seat in the park under a tree. I sat down on it and watched her walk away. My head hurt. It was full of her words. She was Jim's girlfriend until he met me. Was that true? Why didn't he tell me? And he played music in a band . . . Was that true as well? I thought I knew Jim, but now . . . I didn't know what to believe or to think. I only knew that I was afraid. Very afraid. I knew why Jim never spoke to me about his music. Because I'm deaf.

Just then I felt my phone ring. I took it from my bag and looked at it. There was a text message from Jim.

I didn't answer the message.

Mum looked at me when I arrived at Busy Kids. 'Are you all right, Sam?' she asked me. 'You look ill.'

'I'm OK,' I signed and I took the shopping into the kitchen where we make the children's lunches. Mum followed me.

'Sam?' she said. 'What is it?'

I didn't want to talk about it. But Mum's face was very worried, so I told her.

'You must speak to Jim,' she said. 'Do you want me to phone him?'

'No,' I said. 'No, thank you. I need to think.'

I was sad all day. No, I was worse than sad. My happy world was broken into pieces.

At four o'clock, Mum told me to go home early. 'I've got a friend coming for dinner, but I'm busy here,' she said. 'Can you cook something?'

I was happy to go home early, but I wasn't hungry. But I made a pizza for Mum and her friend.

Mum got home at six o'clock and went to have a shower. When somebody comes to the front door at our house, the lights go on and off. Then I know that someone's there. The lights in the kitchen went on and off while I was making a salad and Mum was in the shower. I went to the front door to see who it was.

I could see a man through the glass. It was Jim.

I opened the door. He was smiling, but I couldn't smile back. I was pleased to see him, but I was sad too, because of the meeting with the girl.

'Hi, Sam,' he said. 'These are for you.' Then I saw he had some flowers. Beautiful flowers. Red roses, lots of them. Flowers for a boyfriend to give to his girlfriend. But in my head I saw the girl from the party in her red dress. The roses were the same colour as her dress. Did Jim give *her* roses when he was her boyfriend?

'Thank you.' I took the flowers from him, and when I looked up again, Jim was saying something. Except of course I didn't know what it was. I don't think I have ever felt so sad about being deaf as at that moment.

Jim took the flowers back from me and put them down on a table inside the house. Then he put his arms around me. I knew he was trying to *show* me what he wanted to say to me. It was the same thing as his text message, the same thing as the roses: 'I love you.'

I was happy that Jim loved me. But I was still sad because I knew love wasn't enough.

Chapter 9 *Pizza and talking*

When I was about fifteen years old, my favourite books and films were all love stories.

The stories were all the same. There was a man (the hero) and a woman (the heroine). They met. But there was always a problem which meant they could not be together at first. Perhaps the hero was hurt by love in the past and didn't want a girlfriend now. Or the heroine had an important job and didn't have time for a boyfriend. Anyway, these books or films always finish in the same way. The hero and the heroine know that they are in love, so the problems aren't important. The only important thing is their love. When we tell children stories we often finish, 'and they were happy ever after'. It's the same with love stories. The hero and the heroine are always 'happy ever after'. Happy together always, with no problems.

But real life is different to stories, and I'm not a heroine. Anyway, I read hundreds of those books when I was fifteen, and there was never a story about a deaf girl with a boyfriend who played music.

I moved away from Jim as Mum came down the stairs. Her hair was wet, but she was smiling at Jim. I soon saw that he was the 'friend' coming to dinner.

'I don't want you to be sad,' she signed to me while Jim put the roses in some water, 'so I phoned Jim and asked him to dinner. After we've eaten, you can tell him why you're sad. And until then, I can find out more about him.'

She was smiling like the children in the Busy Kids nursery smile sometimes. When they've done something a little bad. I don't usually feel angry with the children, and I couldn't feel angry with Mum.

While we ate the pizza, Jim and Mum talked. Mum laughed a lot. I knew she liked Jim. Of course she liked Jim. Sometimes Mum signed to me to tell me what she and Jim were talking about: his studies at university, his family, her days as a musician with the Sweet Pepper Band.

'Jim's father plays guitar,' she told me. 'He was quite famous when he was a young man. Isn't that interesting?'

Mum was like a young girl. She was having fun talking to Jim. But I sat quietly, watching them. I didn't eat very much. I wasn't hungry. I think Mum was asking Jim more questions about his family. But I just felt sad that I didn't already know about his father being a famous musician.

After two months of being Jim's girlfriend I didn't know his father was a famous musician. I didn't know about Jim playing in a band. And I didn't know that the girl from the party was his girlfriend before me.

What else didn't I know?

'I'm going out now,' Mum said to me after dinner. 'I'll wash the plates when I come home. You stay here and talk to Jim.'

I saw her say goodbye, and then she left.

I took Jim's plate. 'Do you want a coffee?' I asked him.

'No, thank you,' he said. He was looking at me, waiting, but I didn't know what to say or how to begin. I only knew that I wanted to *sign* to him what I was thinking and feeling. I wanted him to understand signing. Signing is my first language and I wanted to talk to him about the girl from the party in my first language.

Jim waited until I was looking at him. 'Your mum told me what happened,' he said. 'She told me about Lauren.'

So, I thought, *that's* what she's called. Lauren. I didn't like her and I didn't like her name.

'Sam,' Jim said, 'Lauren wasn't my girlfriend when you and I met at the party. We did go out together for a few months, but that was last year. We're just friends now. Or we *were* friends. Oh, I'm so angry with her for hurting you!'

I didn't think Jim would lie to me. But he didn't tell me about his music . . .

Jim knew what I was thinking. 'I'm sorry I didn't tell you about my music,' he said.

'You didn't tell me because it's a problem,' I said, but he didn't agree.

'No,' he said, 'that's not true.'

'Yes, it is,' I said.

I told him he loves music and I can't hear music. It's a big problem. I told him he doesn't want a deaf girlfriend, he wants a hearing girlfriend.

But now Jim couldn't understand me. I wasn't speaking very well because I was angry and sad. So I wrote it down for him: 'You want a girlfriend who can hear your music. I'm not good for you.'

Jim's face was very sad. 'Don't say that,' he said. 'It isn't true. I know what I want, and that's you. You *are* good for me, Sam. You're very good for me.'

When I didn't answer, Jim started to write again: 'I want to be with you, Sam.'

'I want to be with you too.' That's what I *wanted* to write. But I didn't, because I couldn't forget Lauren's words.

Maybe Jim *did* want me. Maybe Lauren just wanted to hurt me. But her words were true. I could never know Jim, the man who played music. So, could I ever really know Jim?

Chapter 10 *Jim's band*

Jim went home after that. I told him to go because I needed to think. Before he went, he wrote something down and gave it to me. I read it after he left.

It said: 'I believe that sometimes it's more important to feel than to think. We love each other. Don't forget that.'

I didn't forget it. I thought about it all the time. But I also remembered Lauren's words. And Jim's music. It was the worst time of my life.

Mum knew I was sad. 'Take a holiday from work, Sam,' she told me. 'Visit Ron in London.'

I thought it was a good idea. I always had fun with Ron. So I went.

But it's difficult to have fun with anyone when your world is in pieces. I was in London, not Norwich, but I still was thinking about Jim; I wasn't having fun at all. And I soon saw that Ron and his friend Mary were boyfriend and girlfriend now, not just friends.

Ron felt bad about Jim and me. He tried not to be too happy about Mary when I was there. He didn't want me to feel worse. But every time he looked at her, he smiled. And I understood. Of course I understood! Until a week ago it was the same for me. I felt happy every time I looked at Jim. But not any more . . .

A few days later, when it was time for me to catch the train home, Ron took me to the station. We stood together on the station platform with hundreds of people hurrying to work around us.

Ron signed to me, 'Sam, I don't think of you as my deaf friend,' he said. 'I think of you as my kind, funny friend. I'm sure it's the same for Jim.'

'I'm so lucky to have you as my friend,' I told him.

We kissed and said goodbye, and then I got on the train. I wanted to believe Ron, but Lauren's words were always in my head: 'Jim wants to be with someone who can hear his music.' I knew it was true.

When I got home Mum looked at me. She saw in my face that nothing was different. 'Send Jim a text message, Sam,' she said. 'Please. Speak to him. I hate to see you like this.'

'I can't,' I told her.

She looked at me for a long time. 'Do you know what I think?' she said. 'I don't think this is about Jim at all. I think it's about your father.'

I looked at her, but I didn't say anything. I wanted to know what she meant.

'I didn't want to tell you this,' she said, 'but now I think it's best.'

Mum's face was sad, and I felt afraid.

'What is it?' I asked.

She closed her eyes for a moment. 'Your father left us because he met another woman: a woman who didn't have any children and who thought your father was wonderful. She didn't want to play guitar or have children. She only wanted to be with him. Sam, your father didn't leave because you were deaf. He left because he didn't want to be a father to *any* child.'

Mum was very sad now. She was crying and her face was

wet. I wanted to put my arms around her, but she started signing again.

'You think Jim will leave you after a few months because you're deaf. But I think you're wrong. Jim isn't the same as your father. He doesn't just think about himself. He's a good man and he loves you.' She smiled at me. 'Oh, Sam, I understand, I really do. When you love somebody you feel afraid. But it's better to feel afraid than to feel sad. Sometimes you have to fight for what you want.' She put her arms around me and soon we were both crying. Then, after a few minutes, she smiled at me. She looked happy now, like Mum again.

'Get your coat,' she told me. 'I know where Jim is. We can go to see him.'

I didn't ask any questions, I just did what she said. I wanted to see Jim. I wanted to see him very much.

Mum drove through the city centre. I didn't know where we were going or how she knew where Jim was. I was busy thinking about love stories and about the problem keeping me from Jim.

It wasn't that I was deaf and it wasn't because my dad left when I was born. It was me. I was making problems because I was afraid. I was fighting against something I really wanted, and it was stupid. I could never kill my love for Jim; it was too strong.

After ten minutes the car stopped and I saw we were near a church. But Mum didn't go into the church, she went up to the building next to it, St Mark's Church Hall.

Before she opened the door, I stopped her. 'How did you know where to find Jim?' I asked her.

Mum smiled. 'I came here while you were in London,' she said and smiled again. 'Follow me. It's all right.'

Then she opened the door and went in. After a moment I went in after her. And there was Jim with four other men. They were playing music, and I knew this was Jim's band.

Jim was playing drums. There were four drums of different sizes. Jim was playing all of them. His hands were moving very quickly. Quicker than Mum's hands when she's speaking to me. I watched him play for a few moments. At first he didn't see me, but I was happy just to look at him. It was very good to see him again. And now I was *really* seeing him. Because this was the Jim who played music: this was the *real* Jim.

Chapter 11 *Happy ever after*

I knew the music was loud because I felt the vibration of the sound in the floor under my feet. Mum put her hands over her ears.

When Jim saw me there was not as much vibration because he stopped playing his drums. He got up and walked over to me and his friends stopped playing too. I think everyone was looking at us, but I'm not sure. All I remember is Jim's smile and the love in his eyes before he kissed me.

As I kissed him back, I forgot to be afraid. This was Jim and I loved him. There was nothing to be afraid of.

After a few moments he moved about a metre away and started to sign to me. He made some mistakes, but I understood. Just as he understood when I spoke to him. And I remembered his fast hands on the drums . . .

There was no problem.

This is what he signed to me: 'Your mum taught me some sign language. Now I'll teach you to play drums. Come with me.'

Before I could answer, Jim took my hand in his. We moved to stand with his friends. Mum was smiling at me. Everyone was smiling.

Jim stood behind me and his hands were on my hands and then I was playing the drums. And the vibration travelled from the drums to my hands and up my arms to my head. It was wonderful.

As wonderful as my small hand on the front of Mum's guitar.

Cambridge English Readers

Look out for these other titles in the series:

Level 2

Logan's Choice
by Richard MacAndrew

'I'm Inspector Logan of the Edinburgh police,' Jenny said. 'I'm very sorry about the death of your husband.'

Who killed Alex Maclennan? His friend, his wife or her brother? It isn't easy, but Logan has to choose.

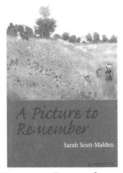

A Picture to Remember
by Sarah Scott-Malden

Cristina Rinaldi works for the Museo Nacional de Bellas Artes in Buenos Aires. She loves art and is happy with her life. Then one day she has a motorbike accident and can't remember some things. But there are two men who think she remembers too much, and they want to kill her before she tells the police what she saw.

The Double Bass Mystery
by Jeremy Harmer

Penny Wade is a musician. She is enjoying her first visit to Barcelona with her orchestra. But first her double bass is lost, and then someone in the orchestra dies. The police want to know what happened and Penny's life changes as she also slowly learns the truth.

Jojo's Story *by Antoinette Moses*

'There aren't any more days. There's just time. Time when it's dark and time when it's light. Everything is dead, so why not days too?'

Everyone in Jojo's village is dead, and Jojo is alone.

46

Level 3

The House by the Sea
by Patricia Aspinall

Carl and Linda Anderson buy a weekend house by the sea. But one weekend Linda does not arrive at the house, and Carl begins to worry. What has happened to her?

The Ironing Man
by Colin Campbell

While Tom is at work in London, his wife Marina is left bored at home. She wishes for someone to do the housework for her and the Ironing Man enters her life. Soon everything begins to change for Marina and Tom.

Double Cross
by Philip Prowse

Secret agent Monika Lundgren chases a would-be killer, and meets a mysterious football team, a rock musician, and a madman with dreams of world power . . .

The Lahti File
by Richard MacAndrew

'Foreign executive' Ian Munro is sent to Lahti in Finland to investigate some strange events. When the man he is there to meet is killed in front of him, Munro starts looking for answers and discovers a poisonous secret.

The Beast *by Carolyn Walker*

'You may see something moving in the corner of your eye . . . I am following in the darkness behind you. I am your worst dream.'

On holiday in Wales, Susie meets the 'undead'. Is it a man or an animal?

Two Lives *by Helen Naylor*

In the small Welsh village of Tredonald, Megan and Huw fall in love. But is their love strong enough to last? Death, their families and the passing years are all against them.

A Puzzle for Logan
by Richard MacAndrew

'Someone's found a young woman's body in Holyrood Park. We're wanted over there immediately.'

Did an escaped murderer kill the woman? Or somebody else? Can Logan find the answer to the puzzle?

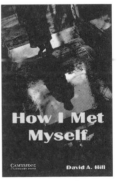

How I Met Myself
by David A. Hill

In a dark street in Budapest, John Taylor meets someone who changes his life. But who is this man? And what is he trying to tell John?